LIONESS

Chérie Taylor Battiste was born in London in 1976. After graduating from SOAS University of London, she worked as a TV researcher before moving on to acting, winning the Norman Beaton Fellowship, joining the BBC Radio Drama Company and gaining various parts on stage and screen. Alongside this, she facilitated workshops in prisons and schools, going on to project manage the embedding of creative learning in schools with CapeUK.

Finding herself a lone parent of two, as austerity hit, she returned to poetry, her first means of expression during her challenging childhood. She saw poetry as freedom, a rare opportunity to have an uncensored cultural voice, and a way of sharing her unique set of experiences. Find her on Twitter @LionessPoet.

LIONESS

CHÉRIE TAYLOR BATTISTE

Valley Press

First published in 2019 by Valley Press
Woodend, The Crescent, Scarborough, YO11 2PW
www.valleypressuk.com

First edition, first printing (March 2019)

ISBN 978-1-912436-14-9
Cat. no. VP0134

Edited by Wendy Pratt and Jo Haywood.
Text design by Jamie McGarry.
Cover photograph by Sophie Rackett.
Cover design by Jamie McGarry and Chérie Taylor Battiste.

Printed and bound in the EU by Pulsio, Paris.

LOTTERY FUNDED

Supported using public funding by
ARTS COUNCIL
ENGLAND

Contents

This is Not a Poetry Collection 9

Horse with Laughter 10

Little Gollywog 13

Maypole 14

It Comes in Waves 23

Baobab 24

Strid & Chez 26

Black Pepper 36

What They Didn't Know 41

Two Cities 45

I Am Here 50

Annette 53

Sugarcane 54

Saltfish Fritter 57

Back Home 59

Dunns River Falls 63

Lioness 64

Tower Block Coltrane 67

Us 68

Inn Saei 69

Witholding Breath 72

Rings 75

It's Not Me It's London 76

Metamorphosis 77

Several Days 80

Ripe Fruit 84

Salve 85

Semaphore 86

Kintsugi 1 88

Kintsugi 2 90

Kintsugi (金継ぎ, "golden joinery") is the Japanese art of repairing broken pottery with lacquer dusted or mixed with powdered gold, silver or platinum. It treats breakage and repair as part of the history of an object, that adds to its value, rather than something to disguise.

This is Not a Poetry Collection

It's a rewriting
A resetting
An ultrasound
of a consciousness
birthed in me
worth not forgetting

This is new blood
This is blood letting
Blood giving

A raw truth sieving
to suture a future

A new body of work
A search for a new living

A removal of curled up hurt
A cutting of regretting
Opening of valves that salve
to a woke coming-round setting

A recovery from
cultural conditioning
A gender agenda sedation

This is a celebration
of a successful soul operation

Horse with Laughter

I remember the way she laughed
as the horse suddenly cantered
and her nerve pathways faltered
her slowly slipping around the peaty down
of its round belly
as flies buzzed like giddy girls
her tendons slackened
her trousers gathered
around Aberdeen-thick calves
the leather saddle's creaking sound
her laugh deep and boundary-less
despite the illness
that could have slowly
dragged us all to the ground

In the end
hanging upside down
tangled in stirrups buried
amongst meadow flowers
and mole hills

the way she giggled

Sorry
Sorry

the contrast as bold as the smell of Christmas
in the August heat from the pines
her eyes darting to me with reassurance
laughing even more
until we couldn't talk

the irony
she repeated the phrase

I'm fine
I'm fine

she was who she was
the boarding school baby
who didn't get to go home in the holidays
who would sleep soundly on rock
during the rare camping excursions

Thick skin
Scar tissue
or both

She just laughed

at all the ways that strangers stared
whenever her limbs gave way

smile still beaming
a buttercup on a crushed stem
not knowing
the continents she had tasted

More fool them
she'd say
hushed
More fool them

and because she laughed away
judgements on her disability

I was less crippled
by their judgment
of me

Black daughter of white mother
their inability to see

Sameness through the
different ways
we were 'other'

Now that my mum is gone

When I think of when
the illness started
when her health became
a horse already bolted
what is left
is the way she took
me riding anyway
just after diagnosis

she was tethered
to her love for me
and paced me with her calm
and how she unmothered
mothered me
but even more
I remember the boldness
of her laughter
and the grace of its balm

Little Gollywog

They loved me
but called me
little gollywog

would dress me to impress
like a princess doll
in matching coats and hats
styling a white glazed vision
on me
as black invention

Fate
fashionably late
staged an intervention as I left
another foster home
intact

Maypole

The first day at my new primary school
they did a maypole dance

I held stance in the middle with the pole
trembling in my soul
as I realised
for the first time
I was a minority

they seemed all blonde
suddenly
skipping
       weaving
            songs
seemed like a secret sorority

no "Hey Fatty Bum Bum"
with patois via Yorkshire twang
no double dutch skipping song
my old school friends sang

no afros no cornrow plaits
their hair leapt and flipped
the more freely they danced

the tighter I gripped

flying ribbons
wove a rainbow tent
bent low
under a blanket of hues
confused by my first

otherness bruise
somehow knowing
I'd be flying
different colours too

my white friends told me
Teacher spoke to me
in a different way
no language to say
she was prejudiced or racist
but they helped me to place this
feeling that lingered like smoke
infusing the words she spoke
the disdain
that would
shift to disgust in her eye
my resolution

to never cry

I am textbook torn
I am the splitting, bending nib
of a fountain pen
ink jamming
shrinking small
to fit the margins fast
my black drying out
like finger stains
I am a smudged
blot in the white of her class

no play or rainbow colours in
the wall I build around myself

she offers only whitewashed bricks
unforgiving sticks and stones
breaking my identity's bones

drinking in the taste of race
with my morning milk
in painful little sips

watching as she extends
her neck too straight
stretching superiority
unnaturally from its nape
she asks a question

words cower on my lips

Future me learns reason
I can't see myself
am sightless
of way to free myself
is shackled to the same empire flash
that blinded
back
at Africa's rape
atomic bomb of anthropology
a toxic trace of distortions
of race will follow me

yet without apology
daily
she pulls the switch

enrobed in entitlement gone rogue
Sometimes she wore a uniform
khaki with crisp folds

barbed with empire's garbs
naked in emperor's
new clothes
the safari suit still fits

without knowing in sewing class
I'm tearing my colours
from her maypole mast
As I weave
she looms
behind me
It's too soon for her
too fast
she can't quite interlace
that I do the Dutch girl we're embroidering
with a brown face

she tells me Dutch 'coloureds' don't exist
despite Boers being
first at the Cape

This is the only thing I confess
to my white adoptive mum
protecting her body that's sick
from rejecting stress
but she unstitches the bitch
untangles the mess
Teacher succumbs

there is a banner her privilege flies
to avoid looking in my eyes
where cross stitches are mapped
on her side
it's nostalgia
for colonial times
justified by ugly lies about all that's black

on my side of the banner
that for centuries
has blown silent
is a constant hurt that fans
the twisted needlework of truth
of history's evil work
like a black Bayeux Tapestry

but more violent

These threads of race
won't break
woven in my now
they persist
pride and brown thread intwined
I am mannequin stuck with
the fabric of her fear

I resist

colonies cotton makes her ears deaf
I deny her from weaving that
blindfold before my eyes

As she asks me
"What happens to a tadpole"
I said "metamorphosis"
aware she wanted the answer
that it turned into a frog
to dwarf her myth
that black equates with "thick"
I bait her
with intellectual traits
she can't negate
black self paled
I still wagged her tail
as she failed
to make me her dog

She fears
I am native in revolt
when I choose Ethiopia for my project
(an auto black default
setting reaching out for what I'm not getting)

she plays with a cold stare
her eyes burn through
the back of my dress
with need to suppress

frame rigid
austere

face fixed
as the images of grass skirts
and mud huts in the book
I am reading

She would not be here
were it not for women
with mahogany skin
and full thighs
pin-pricked pride still bleeding
as I edit her lessons' lies

future me would study
ancient scripts
Ethiopia's colonial resistance
future me would understand
the sweet irony
of her need for distance from fact

my project choice
was the birthplace of man
her "Heart of Darkness"
would spark
a black blaze in me

The fact her race
could imprison
themselves
in the colour of my face
to escape seeing who I am

with the maypole of my soul
flying red gold and green
I now sit bold and seen
aware that I am other

As the next child of colour came
whichever twisted nostalgia she claimed
to legitimise tying them
in the ribbons of Enoch's wrath
she'd know they too
may fly their own colours
at the top of her class

Teacher now serves cream teas
and is a pillar of the community
the damaging dose of prejudice
her teutonic impunity
started my search
for a tonic
an immunity
from racism to swallow
I knew there was a playground
with a black sun to follow

she herself in a way sent me to SOAS
to my birth-family to Africa and Jamaica
she made my theme song

Young Gifted and Black

I saw black pride shine on Nina Simone
and that she knew how to renew
through what didn't break her

No longer alone
my own ink spewed
and overwrote
Teacher's red pen

No more denying
I started flying
my own colours
let the maypole go
as my orange hibiscus print skirt flowed
as I wound rounding hips and pranced
at the Northern School

bliss in each twist
as I studied Caribbean dance

I did my homework
on how my soul worked
started to wedge achievement
in the schisms
envisaged an afrofuture
where I'd have the chance to advance
and honoured my mission
of a pledge to revision
my Black girl in
White world circumstance

It Comes in Waves

Embracing riptides of attack
has buoyed me
more than staying at shore could

displacing waves that push you back
can turn and save you
pulling you forward

Baobab

Ten years old
school playground
I'm needing the scene to change
a respite from fresh pain

so I pray for fresh rain
to retreat inside to a warm seat
play a board game
hide

Keep the same despite
the red haired boy with red raged cheeks
whipping me with words
for not being white

somewhere something redwood big
must keep falling in his life

Nigger-monkey-bitch
Horror movie glitch
Repeats
the black character always dies first
Eyes immersed in Kickers on my feet

they bully my bully
in his too-small-Poundstretcher-clothing
knowing it'll linger
he redirects the finger
they point
shouting
ginger

To me
passing on the self-loathing
cuts my roots

So his own rot isn't seen
burying it with my branches

I'm uprooted
Ugly baobab tree

Eighteen years old
He chats me up
His mind decolonised
Black not demonised
but being vandalised
is carved into my bark
whip scarred down my spine
a backdrop to the unkind
a cinema in my mind

me and baobab are both important nothings
It stores water
I store cultures that collide
I'm another mother's daughter

somewhere her brown mask cracks
remembering my eyes
so I leap
catching missing heartbeats
as I reach for a tribe

Strid & Chez

I first saw Astrid in the garden
of her dad's cottage

she spoke bright strong words
her hair matched the yellow clematis

we became friends one morning
both late for school
early for life

Switching out
the pleasantries
like swapping sandwiches
She said 'my mum has hepatitis'
I replied
'my mum has multiple sclerosis'
And the scary names paled

Something registered
as we missed register

the torn safety nets slowed
as they trembled about us

we somehow reassembled
as assembly groaned on without us

then in netball
marking each other
disposable players
sent for better balls
squeezing toady-skinned
terracotta rubber

I said ooh it's like testing
melons in Safeway's

we laughed
with the humour
of clever girls
needing a break from
knowing too much

we called the others 'trees'
with their smooth lives
uniform branches
sliding down norms
whilst we were debating about
Apartheid
Northern Ireland
Thatcher

I can't see the wood
for the trees we'd whisper
as we'd slip away from groups
never dragged into
the soup of nay sayers
who bragged about
their parents' CD players

on Saturdays we'd
shop then cook
pretending
loudly
I was
an African princess
she a white lady in waiting

as we bought incongruous ingredients
and on the way home
as the old woman opposite
glared through a shield of nets
Astrid would ask
with enough volume to get through
loose fitting panes

'Are you looking for the bone
through her nose or the grass skirt'

enough to get me through
my tight fitting pain
the bare realities

of race anticipated
aware of the British
in the bulldog we baited

we both had mothers who shrugged off
the shoulder padded
blouses of the times
whose rejections of norms
were scrawled on
dog eared Post-it notes
stuck on our outsides
that we internalised

there would be
no blue mascara
in our lives

after drum lessons
we'd find songs in storms
paradiddling in puddles
outside her house
pounding value into
unbelonging to norms
dancing lioness into our mouse

we'd talk like talking might end
as if it had limits

every 59 minutes
we'd power steal
cheating BT's
under an hour deal

one night
I kept dreaming
her mother had died

I was woken by her call
and wept as she
told me she had

she didn't cry
we never questioned
that at the cliff edge

we were psychic bungy tied
I ran to her to find
that sips of tea
were as much as she
could swallow from me

her eyes were a corridor
flooded with sadness

her shadow essence
floating foetal at the back

but built of Irish stone
the house of her soul
didn't collapse

running home
reaping over the grim
guilty and grateful my mum
whose limbs were
falling to bits
remained

I was sobbing so hard
into her awkward arms
she wobbled on her
Maori walking sticks
the mother of pearl eyes watched
embedded in the grain

when my parents were away
and the man Astrid said
made her believe in evil
stood with a knife to my chest

my mind was dismembered from my body
I remembered
the Ripper's girl

murdered on the same Wood Lane
that linked our homes

like an artery
feathered with trees that whispered
the bloody secrets of
what can happen to girls like Us

girls like them
too much too soon
knowing some clematis
never bloom in the shadows
that loom around those men

and just as
no emotion
no heart race
became a slow motion
other worldly place
she rang the phone

just as the tip of the blade
dimpled my skin
piercing his bubble
enough to let me answer

her only words
are you ok?

my only word
no

and she came
running like she
never did in netball

my mind running over

will he let me open the door?

without pause he did
without words we ran
back along the artery
to her dad's house
me hiding in the basement
waiting for inevitability
of a shadow cast against
the tiny stone window
hearing her claiming ignorance
knowing her pitiful poker face
remembering all he'd done
imagining what he might do

but I slipped through the small space
like I was nothing
because I was nothing

she was forever a witness
reminding me
I wasn't weak
that after the bruises healed
I could stop being
swollen with blame
that there was no shame sealed
in the trauma of what broke me

in the well-watered fear
that trailed behind me
and choked me
like bindweed
for years
and years

and years later
she returned from overseas
when my netball had no air
just in time to sit with me
in the days waiting
for my mother to pass
widening my stance
to catch the hurt

she came
she made tea
I could swallow more
than those sips
I could digest
The nourishment she shared
that my mother knew my children
that hers never had

from anyone else
cold comfort
but not from her

we cupped our hands around everything
found warmth in all the winters
and being there all along

she believed me when I said
I'd prepared to
be able to bear the blow
for my mum

that I would be able to
take the point of the blade
that somehow
we were still the punctured netballs
refusing to lose more air

that we would forge nets as we leapt
nets that let clematis grow
till it reeled around steel hoops

we fetched ourselves
running to each other
using our punctured pasts
to keep our own children
wonderfully inflated
believing what's ruptured
can bounce back
cushioned by selves
resuscitated

now we are matriarchs
of our own teams

we mark each other
our mother's daughters
the girls wearing tabards
but objecting to the rules

of the match
teasing out the good bits
with ease
tending to the wood
accepting the fact
that we don't give a shit
if we don't fit
with the trees

Black Pepper

I watch
with sell-out guilt
Burning
as the police take him

seeing how many of them there are
knowing they're needed
but that because they
come to the right side
of this urban valley
the white side
makes their high numbers tally

there's a crazy black man
running amok
hue leaking out
what they already knew
about have nots

People peep through nets

no one gloats

Just sharks to

stark new smell

on strangled throat

bruises swell
with what wells unsaid

Dad's head seeps
blood
bell pepper red

It's all wrong here
Nothing is right

This crushed black pepper girl
is nestled in a pestle world
of marble white

five men prize him away
but the kernel of him
eternally under my skin
can't be un-wrenched

later
numbers to get through
the emergency switchboard
bleed ink in the sweat of my hand
I don't think to unclench
forget it's mine
next time he will be
dragged from my school
after he hits my teacher
before I sit my exam

I'm compartmentalised now
He is sectioned

So I'll get an A
because I can

Nothing and everything
scares me now
after the not dyings
nothing compares now

I'm trapped in this autumn
Trying not to fall
I should be a whole pepper tree
new leaves uncurled
not cracked open to dust
I may as well stay grey

now my black shell's curve
has white inside
splayed open
May just stay grey
and token
in this monochrome mistrust

I watch counsellor number one's
face flinch as I share my story
She is white
She is retired
She says

as I talk
she becomes
Whiter
she is fragile
I protect her
I don't tell her the worst bits
she can't do anything for me
she says

I don't give her grief
It stays with me
I keep it
I need it
to cushion the pain
of her relief
to cover
my unrecovering belief

counsellor number two's
face does not flinch
I am glad

he's in his late thirties
and black

his face also does not flinch
as he declares he's attracted to me
It's wrong
but nothing is right

I try to see through
his refracted light

to the fractions left of me
to the schoolgirl I am
but can't seem to be
hoping only that he drives me
in his convertible one day
that shiny things will
make *me* convertible one day
will wash away the taint
so school friends see

me a different kind of black
blinded by the paint of
a midlife-crisis-car
shade of red

he's only telling me
in the spirit of honesty

he says

but my spirit is
no longer dwelling in me
it left in the traumas
I'm here to talk about
something the somebodies
haven't thought about

after years unspoken
the fear clenched fists
will be uncurled

it will come to be
my oyster

this cracked world
With the right therapist
PTSD tangles are untied
As with wisdom I open
I see I'm not
crushed black pepper girl

I'm black pearl
Unbroken inside

What They Didn't Know

They were so sure
that I was the hired help
for my mum

As a child I would walk
carrying her bags
as she held sticks

as a teenager I shifted nervously
behind her badly-driven scooter
later
adjusting straps to hold her head up
to keep her feet on

and I would see other people in wheelchairs
or walking with sticks
with women of colour
scaffolding their weakened limbs
patiently repeating slowed words

flavouring their caring duties
with the nuances of missed homelands

and I would understand
how they could think that
but I'd be too tired
to unpack all the concepts
tired from all the times
my dad and I would get out of the car
at the supermarket
and the shoppers would
keep staring right
through their resentment

I was staring back
box solid and flat-pack-quick
in constructing judgement
despite their wet cardboard spines
sure that they knew
some sordid take
on the older white man
with the too-young-too-black-girl

ensuring I would not
kiss him goodbye
in public

I would watch them
sharp edged and cubed
from proudly shuffling
to the backs of their boxes
creased by categories
but still comfy in concepts

the same people would
release too-loud-tuts
assuming my mum was drunk

then on seeing my black face
juxtaposed with her white
rosy-nosed Scottish one
They watched us
crane-like
reminding me constantly
that my birth story had no stork

They didn't know
since finding her
after school
collapsed by the back door
in the snow

I'd prayed each night to the big Jesus
in the grounds of the convent
at the back of our house
that glowed impossibly white
against the night

That once the nuns
at their summer fair
stared at my colour like the rest
I'd pray to my own god
for resurrection
as an animal able to survive
the hunter in all their eyes

They didn't know that the anger
was because I was carefully cradling
each day their staring soiled us
as one more chance
to show her
that she was my earth
and to hide from her

the fact that I was falling away
at the slow crumbling of her

They didn't know
that my unboxable self
would sift through
their ideas of me
like sand
to cushion us both
when she finally fell

so sure of what they knew

they didn't know that

Two Cities

I step onto a nearly empty tube train
and find a seat
without stain

I catch the eye of woman
a seat away
with an uncanny
resemblance to Thatcher

she grabs her bag
from the seat between us
I assume she's assuming
I'll hatch a plan
to snatch what I can

I'm dressed well
but can tell
I won't dislodge the
idea from her head
that I am the Artful Dodger
with other hue
like Dickens
plot thickens
as she stews
thinking
I'll pick a pocket or two

I sit still the moment loaded
ignoring everyone
is the coded behaviour that saves you

the train remains moving
through the next station

until an alarm sounds
and the boundary she found
is eroded

my eyes dip
then suddenly she
sits down beside me
the humility she thought she forgot?
maybe it was inside
the bag all along

the tube's stopped at a station marked fear
we're both humbled and human
believing our final destination is near

It's too close to 9/11
to not acknowledge
that the detonation
would bring the same ash
make a snow dome
tomb of the semi-circle
curve of the carriage
mirroring her u-turn swerve
I atone my tone to tender
from disparaged

same station of Kings
still marked with
a cross from the fire
I'm sweating
she probably just perspires

the doors open to actual smoke
the tannoy tells us not to leave
I breathe what may be
the choking punchline
to fate's race relations joke

she may be the last person I see

panic now
this lady *is* for turning
she realigns with
reality that ability to survive
trumps any disparities in earnings
asking what's happening

I say we'll just wait
it negates any feelings about
her face
her earlier rejection
the connection reaffirming
and that about face
between hers and mine

there's a myriad of
complexities beyond complexion
I change track to the direction
of a universal place
we're both somebody's somebody
so I ask about family
she tells me about her son's selection
his school team place
the way he runs like his dad
same measured pace

together we pour on water
I say my brother was at LSE
turns out at the same time as her daughter

in the end we're talking with ease
in a short time we believe
London is burning
The difference she was spurning
becomes a shared reference point

leaning in as we're learning
not shouting fire fire
just smoke and mirrors
the rules we're flouting
they get thinner
as there's no doubt in
how deftly we left
the thought
no exit
meant we'd expire
because the sameness we sift
drifts us from tired ideas
that we're entirely different kinds
and puts out the fear of being
trapped in the underground pyre
that burned through our minds

suddenly
back in motion
the panic is passed

Dynamic lasts
changed

There's sanity in the notion
that for a moment
the madness of separate
worlds rearranged

She stands to leave
smiles and thanks me
I pass her the bag
whose importance
outranked me
hoping she tucks
in her purse
a value for the next
black face's worth

I say I think I'll take
the bus the rest of the way
trying to be witty
we laugh
she smiles
we walk away in different directions
with own storyline projections
both with each other's tales
of our two cities

I Am Here

It is not printed on me
this map of the roads I had to take
I just walk bearing my truth
that after bearing me
I lost my bearings

Once I was taken
from her
my mother

when she was gone
and my blackness
couldn't be birthed by her

I realised I would never again
be small enough
to fall into her hands

her long slim fingers
of burnt terracotta
a village unearthed
after I had gone whole cities
the wrong way

because in the spaces
between the races
for the fragmented
there is no right way

No one looks there
They don't have to

because I know
I can't fall into a heap of home
I form my pieces back into pots
fix my cracks with honey and gold
with the lacquer of longing for the lost
hoping they see
beauty in my breaks
the fortitude of my fractures
the memory of magic
in my map of scars

hoping the pots won't hold
the idea that I can't be held
hoping they won't sing with the truth
when their lips are kissed
by the wind

The road is gone
The home is gone

hoping the pot isn't glazed
with the truth I can't bear
that I will always be the child
who was left

the walking alone
peppered with moments
of chameleoning into white
in blizzards of misunderstanding
shaped by shadowing
a blackness of unbelonging
becomes easier than stopping
and asking for directions

because I've always been lost
and what would they say
as the strange cold
numbed their hands
which way would they tell me to go
if I am their only reference point

Because it's not printed on me
This map of the roads I had to take
I just walk bearing my truth

that after bearing me
I lost my bearings
once I was taken
from her
my mother

Annette

she said
As a woman you are eighteen
As a black woman you are a baby

did she know it would be crushing?
my waters muddied?
maybe
the last goodbye before
School of Oriental and African Studies

but my mother's friend Annette
with those words
harsh but honed
made me
like the tight plaits
she always gave me
woven in
long threads
of black pride
hidden inside
I could unwind
through tense binds
of transcultural times
I'd return as black woman
and as she
castor oiled my hair
for my grown-self to plait
I'd share that those words
that uncurled hurt
all those years back
formed the twine
of the rope I climbed
that saved me

Sugarcane

the sight of my siblings' eyes
starts the shredding of
social services files
done with our smiles
and the way our cheeks
all rise the same

paths meet
on this journey
tough and sweet
as sugarcane

this embrace displaces blame
here now to
big-sister-kiss pain
the missing maternal map
once embossed in a face
is washed away as waste
as Lewisham storm djembe plays
percussion on window panes

later we'll have a discussion
see we are not maimed
by society's sores
we are beautiful repercussions
cloaked under
a mother's thunder
her skies of light and dark

more than sparks
there's a brilliance
in our resilience

you can't measure this
finally in the Battiste living room
that's trapped with my past
in the seventies
Grandma's sets of
pearlised peach glass
tea sets grouped
mirroring togetherness

what I know as love grows
in the safe foreverness of fusing with
what's meant for me
back on a path mapped with
unshackled Jamaican Maroon
and Cuban ancestry
the Dunn River's tears
with tracks that can't be traced

and when we smile
our cheeks all rise the same

Here is shelter and primal food
We taste and savour truth

that all roads lead home
to under Grandma's roof
sugaring away bitterness
too sour to eat plain
slow cooked proof
we weren't beaten by the rain

learning curves ahead for miles
Blue-Mountain-steep

but however brief
we'll savour our survival
our smiles and same cheeks
in this reunion relief
on a journey
tough and sweet
as sugarcane

Saltfish Fritter

a guest examining
a saltfish fritter
spies the scotch bonnet pepper
then birds-eyes curled tight
asking *is this your mum?*
whilst testing the heat
with a tiny bite

this important nothing-question
is this your mum?
is hot and new
as the fritter she chews

keeping in sight
the room's elephant
our eyes sifting makeshift
trite answer
drifts to the right answer

tucking away
her eloquence
my Adoptive Mum Tizzy
balancing on MS legs
with grace and
a touch of her waist gives
Marcia my Birth Mum the space

sometimes Marcia fades
forgetting achievements
is displaced

revisiting scorchingly recent
institution-face

This woman
I traced
is my living
breathing
birthplace
she stands shiny as her braids
she doesn't voice or explain
the scalding choice
that Social Services made

the bronze sun dappling her
through the skylight's leafy defence
without grappling with pretence
she whose mind broke
before her waters
singed by the
fire-walk of me being
another mother's daughter
honours the ash
of her experience
into a jewel to adorn her
as she answers
unfazed
with important-nothing phrase

this is the woman
that raised Chérie
and I am
the woman that bore her

Back Home

I've given up trying
I'm just kind of being
I've given up looking
I'm just kind of seeing

after the way my
wings were clipped
it's just kind of freeing
to be in Jamaica
and be me

on the journey to a self-made me
I had to cash in the all of me
bet on black and allow
the cultural chips to fall in me
had to trade me

to grow
I needed a chance
to flow and dance
in a sea of skin the same as me
needed to colour enhance
a lack that I felt
statistics made in me

so I peeled off the labels
of wrong and right
good and bad
because if this is
the life I've lived
plain as black and white
it's the one I should have had

so now the light and shade
don't faze me
my learning
won't be undone

it was as if I was a sunbeam
searching storms for
what I could mean
realising all I need to be
is part of the sun

back home I'm shown
that I am Us
and We are one

when in Kingston I see
my double
with same face and eyes
I watch a man at Ochi market
carve a mango seed into
a face who's a spirit you can read

then with tides
calm as my people's pace
and steady as sound systems' bass
waves splash diamonds
on each child's face

human nature reaches out
bleaches out history's ties
despite the developing-world thirst
in the driest cracked earth
we burst through with our worth

and hibiscus thrive
my journey is blessed with tests
rests as lenses
on my eyes
magnifying the
time defying beauty
of the Blue Mountains I see
reminding me my free mind
is edified by
a rebellion defined
Maroon ancestry

when I first meet
my great grandma aged 93
I see the wise well in
the onyx shine
of her blind eyes

sitting in her tiny simple hut
she has the same slim hands
as my mum

Grandma and I
healing
what the separation
had been stealing
by giving my hand
a tiny simple touch

I feel deceived by
the need to leave
no suitcase can
hold the way I'm freed

my spirit is troubled
as it rightly believes
that I am home

bitter sweet
as a tamarind tree
I smuggle a mango
where customs won't see

as more is hidden in me
because now I know
I carry my Jamaica inside
it'll nourish like the yard chicken
and breadfruit from
our family compound that's thriving

a hunger for the taste of home
is now part of me
it's self-satisfying
because there is no more
race to find my place

I've given up trying
I'm just kind of being
I've given up looking
I'm just kind of seeing
after the way my
wings were clipped
it's just kind of freeing
to carry my Jamaica inside
and just be me

Dunns River Falls

I can't quite place it
this love that survives against all odds
iron branded
water swimming in itself one handed
kissing the Gods

I can't quite understand it
the nameless shameless new force of you
when your laughter breaks its banks
pouring a truth
that leaps down the fall of my face
drowning my frowns
so love
waterfalls down

Lioness

the villagers say
until lions write their own history
the tale of the hunt
will always glorify the hunter

the guns they fired didn't miss me
these wounds are no mystery
in fact still the shrapnel blunts
the very teeth and claws
I need to thrive
the urge to re-find my roar
is the synapse surge to survive
I stopped searching for salvation
in hunters' eyes

sinews
in you stay raw
to win you
must realise
till you tend
to your own wounds
you can't tend to
others anymore

so despite unforgiving skies
on this scorched earth
I can still rebirth
in this solitary test
I can bind and thread wounds
with wild ropes of primal hope
I am worth rest
can retreat
be remade

can watch earth's heat
dance vapours as it fades
hear cicadas' symphony
serenade yellow into
pale Serengeti moon
retune as hyenas
silence stars as they croon

as if just for my relearning
soothing the burning with the night's cold
as I lie on a raffia mesh
thickening and firming the matter
that lies within
from broken and thin
to the reaffirmed bold
of brand new flesh

my limbs are rebirthed
and skim cracked red-earth
I leave no tracks back
for past attackers to retread

my supple muscles
are now dense and primed
present and relaxed
after the past tense times

and after being couched in
re-lustred coat of gold
I now trust the
crouched new form
I hold steady
senses tightening

third eye
revisioned

so go tell the hunters to get ready
for their own enlightening
and the stories I saw

as I roar
as lioness arisen

Tower Block Coltrane

Blue Train playing
takes me where you take me

notes in motion
like sparks on tracks
locomotion rhythm
wakes me how you wake me

spine easing melody
you harmonise my back
fingers tap dance on ivory
beckoning the night with its family of stars
jigsaw jazz tessellates with what's inside of me

Blue Train sliding from bar to bar
candlelight makes ebony sculptures dance
smooth arrival
with the glide of the trombone
didn't know where we were going to or why
all I know is the *Blue Train* took us home

Us

We are the generations
with colonial storms
and Windrush still passing us
Eugenics hurricane of old
still unfolds
attempts to loosen our hold
and hijack neural
paths in us

the same wind fuels
the trigger-happy sins
that shoot through
the hearts of glass in us

it seems there's no route through
but you'll still see us frontline
shifting arts and science paradigms
as our pooled diaspora-wide supplies
will be lasting us

the clouds drift as our gifts
lift the present
as we stop carrying
someone else's idea
of our past in us

our light is the black in us
because ancestral flames
like beacons
en masse in us
still flash in us
so pour libations on the feasting-us
that thrives despite
the fasting-us

Inn Saei

Behind this face I have faces
deep beyond what in Iceland they call
the Inn Saei
the sea of the mind

my only beauty lies
in those silent places
but I'm here avoiding eyes
drowning in the times
where thin traces
of my appearance
are seen as my totality

walking down Carnaby Street in 1999
only the seers could see I'm seared
with a please-tear-here
cut and paste plurality
the tremble in my hand
holds such a disparity
from the sureness of my eyes

in this morning's modelling shots
pierced with a pin point that could be real clarity
glossed with the hope of what I'm not

with make-up
they wake up
a false vanity
masking the fact
I was trapped
in thoughts I couldn't stop

I fear this fragility being my finality
but anyway you can't see
in the money shots they got
that I didn't sleep
that this lens

that spirit bends
in a sense keeps
the anxious shell
as the yoke of my soul leaks

broken doesn't sell
as a woman
grabs her man to her
like a dog in need of correction
as I turn down Oxford Street
and I know she's bought into
the myth of misperceived perfection

I ease into the feeling
of this VIP social rejection
suspecting I'm a spectre or a ghost

as she gets to keep the
connection that I want most

I'm in London in
a skin too thin
again wondering
how having
a hand to hold
might complete me
because I'm always alone

but I'm somehow knowing soon
the sea within me
will like a womb
reconstruct me
that I'll shift focus from
this portfolio of defeat

but for now the sea
forms the tears
of a weakened
stuck me

Next meeting
I hide what
they don't seek
they book me
I'm cast
image remains complete
the mask holds fast

Witholding Breath

No one sees how I
seal my mouth when
the waves come down
when the names
and assumptions
bounce all around

Someone told me
they admired that I kept going
after all I'd been through
but black women are strong like that
they said
like there was a choice
in the storms
like the myth that we
are bred and born
rather than *made* resilient

as if we arrive ready for trauma
like we want to dive into rapids

like we're unaware that
people duck faster
at the chips they imagine
flying from our shoulders

and assume we will outlast the
white waves
with our strong words
that we are reinforced
not unendorsed
unheard

Not seeing we must be elastic within
Not men or white
gymnastic in our swim
since the curse
that scattered us
on Atlantic seabed
full as mermaid's purse

said we didn't cry
for milk wet nursed
to babies
who'd grow
to choose to
avoid our eyes

Not only Billie
sang the blues
unaware we are aware of
what we lose
in the tides

Thinking we're static as an old woman
at the edge of a village
created for tourists
a plantation re-enactment
shelved

Thinking we all sit cushioned
in concepts of ourselves
That we somehow had a choice
and chose not to be an easier someone else

Believing that Black Woman
is the things that happened *to* us
intersectionality a subheading
Misogyny and Racism
us making waves
not our constant swim

so I seal my mouth when
the waves come down
then seal it again
to hold my own waves in

Rings

Whatever autumn brings
I let dying leaves fall
distend branches to weather winter winds
but each spring despite the pain
of trying to keep bonsai tight through it all
some things remain forever
rings in the tree of my everythings

It's Not Me It's London

We started with me staring out the fear
of the eyeline of your skyline from Blackheath
in thirteen years of unlucky for some London
you helped sharpen my teeth

The alien flash of the Canary Wharf tower
the saccharine newness neon sweet
but by your vastness classness
humanity-can't-last-ness soured

Found my roar in
your lion country
I had a future mapped
but like all bad relationships
in the end London
you just took much more
than you gave back

Metamorphosis

at times it's seemed caterpillar-slow
the wait to pupate
into this
now in this new sky I boldly spread my wings
and fly
to celebrate my metamorphosis

I felt like another species
the difference dripping out in tears
my black girl journey was forked to a whiter road
I was still with my people
the 200 years
But I was alone
in prejudice on my path

but we were all manacled to the same ideas
the only Black girl in the school
not just the class
my high pitched difference
was mosquitos to my ears

sometimes they see me as a hornets' nest

the way my difference stings
a new black face sells me out
into being an oreo
a coconut
in a white privilege space

but these are not my things

a new white face may assume
a lack of education
a ghetto grace
or with red lipstick on
and showing my curves
then the diva-she-sounds-educated-
but-we-can't-believe-her
glass ceiling occurs
black or white dominoes
or chess
in binaries of race
someone will shift me
back more than a place

so yes I am aware
that my difference stings

but now I no longer smother
the buzzing questions
being the Other Other brings
instead I butterfly through the gales
let them treat me like hornets' nest
when I have already suffered the stings
in my own tale

I refuse to be the fly in ointments
or the fly in soups
and I no longer hoverfly
around societal categories and groups

I am the monarch butterfly
I've travelled many moons back to Me
so with all the facets
on my pearly eyes
it's easy to see why those
who're still bee-bumbling through their fears
fall from the skies distracted with whys
and hows
I gathered such nectar
in my wilderness years

I tell them
at times it seemed caterpillar slow
the wait to pupate
into this
now in a new sky
I boldly spread my wings
and fly
as I celebrate my metamorphosis

Several Days

We
your four children
our faces washed
with the harsh soap of loss
cleaned off
is the banality

can't quite face the finality
but we are there

We are sentries
guarding your room
we greet nurse with a smile
and a hello face
but we're keeping it the space
to be honoured by the grace
of the biggest goodbye
soon

two of my brothers read
me
and my other brother watch your breaths
we gather our flowers to scatter on this test
whilst hoping we don't wilt

sometimes a hug pulls us near
we pull away quick
to catch the tears
elegantly clambering to stand tall again
on your legacy
like stilts
balancing on your every breath
as the axis of our world tilts

it will be several days before
she slips away
the royal-blue-uniformed-doctor on Sunday said
now it's Tuesday night
time for light-blue-nurses
to shift your angle on the bed
to stop the bedsores
it doesn't matter anymore
but I welcome redundant comforting rituals
like offers of coffee
thick with kindness
bitter sweet as a hospital routine
that's become habitual

the hospital routine becomes everything
just as all the everythings are about to change
no more gritting teeth Mum
all the higher powers are lined up
for your release Mum
your peace is worth
this the earth's biggest exchange

nearing the last exhale
your bird frame body's long past
too frail
for this gasping now
I have shared your breaths
the hiss of oxygen somehow
as if you're sailing away
on the sound of waves
the red kite that soared in the days
before sleeps
this night keeps itself
just for us

on this change everything day
like the nights I gave birth
I feel a haze of spirit
that only visits
when life arrives
or is taken away

as if the air is alive
with another world's fireflies
a shine
just a shine
but I just know it's time

and your whole frame
rises again
swelling with the importance
of this last breath

my hands rest
stroking your brow
you taught me how
skimming the widow's peak of your hair
knowing I've long prepared
for only my love
not fear
to be there

and as you go
I throw my words
my love
like flowers
it's the last breath Mum
I know

I'm sure you'll be ok if
I throw
my
love
like
flowers
through this portal
love laced with lily and jasmine
perfuming your shift from the mortal
a daughter's final test
to ensure
you're swaddled
in this nectar nest
wherever you go
so hibiscus honeysuckle lavender
I throw

and I kiss you
once warm
once cold
adjust the blanket
neaten the fold
no regrets
because
all our regrets are already told
and as I leave
I remember all the flower seeds
that you have sowed
whole meadows of love
still inside of me
tender tendrils
that will always grow

Ripe Fruit

the yellow plastic refuse sack
of her things from the hospital
crumpled and defeated
giving up on having a place
as it moves like a rough sleeper
from room to room

I think how much
I don't want to think
about finding it a place
because then she's really no place
so it sits
keeping her with me
as I redo my locs through the night
for the funeral
my hands dance over themselves
grabbing and wrapping
coiled curls straight for a moment
before they disappear back
Neat
Barrelled
Samson
Strength
for tomorrow
saving me from tonight
a meditation a relief
the yellow bag sits
beside me
a ripe fruit of grief

Salve

The space left by my mother
the mother I went to after
I was taken from the mother before
should have been filled
with honey and eucalyptus

grief should have been salved
by something

I was still shaking from first being taken
from the mother I was taken from
who isn't the mother I went to
the mother I went to is gone

Semaphore

I fold into myself
somehow making paper flags
without the triangle
of my two mothers and me

I'm trying to be brave
ensuring my children don't see
the papery broken girl crying
in her paper thin family tree

I'm holding onto the
feeling of her hand
the folds begin to mould
tiny silent tornadoes
to fill and mend
with the same blend of starchy resilience
I was harshly weaned on
the pulped parts
my stop-start story was reeled on

until I am billowing memories of bunting
a patchwork of daughter gratitude
and orphan greed
matrilineal full stop
limp in a lack of release
remembering her blow
the loss of her own mother
the wind whipping away
her time to grieve
the role slipping to me

my end of being
allowed to need
I have my own family's mouths
to paper feed

I become bunting
a silent semaphore
Dancing
Celebrating
Collapsing
Commiserating
confronting the harsh crease

I had a mother
like her
to miss
blessed that she
would kiss
what broke
then tuck it in
a heart shaped envelope
addressed to me
in bold
with love
in each fold

Kintsugi 1

I am black
My glue is gold
and has the shine of insects' wings
I am the pot
dropped as hands forgot to hold
Many impacts sting
In time lapse
I watch myself fold
remoulding implicit
in the exquisite way I implode
I'm not delicate
I am not fixed
Yes sometimes shattered to bits
but mixed up pieces can bend
so I am not fixed
and there is nothing to mend

I tend shape
as landscape after quake
I re-seal to abstract
extract new face
inch by inch
So anyplace can be my plinth
I rinse and buff
No glance back
to form before cracks
resilient mosaic enough
I watch myself unfold
eclipsing prosaic
with brilliance of black and gold
Shape I was meant to be
Beautiful dents in me and dips

Because I am pot dropped
as hands forgot to hold
I'm not delicate
I am not fixed
Yes sometimes shattered to bits
but mixed up pieces can bend
so I am not fixed
and there is nothing to mend

Kintsugi 2

In bits
I am broken but
reassemble to ascend
to form without the trick
of having to pretend
so I am tender with ragged scarring
removing jagged jarring pieces
of ivory towers of those
denying the power
of my hourglass curves
those who on seeing painted lip
from pot want to sip
ignoring it's embossed with
un-glossed unheard words

and I dismiss as suspect
Others who made me Other
as foreign object
who tried to melt as wax
my melanin black
whose flames I swerved

and I pull no punches
with what abusers smashed
as if I was owned
as if I was glass
they themselves had blown

These pieces porous with surrender
have no place they wouldn't render
Pot would rock
would be debased

They have no space in my rebirth
so I lose all isms
and doubt dynamics
fill schisms with truth grout
re-centre my ceramics
rejected pieces I study first
then release far from me
pummel them bury them
taking their thirsty dark from me

In their place
pieces etched with
my son and daughter's face
I carve imprints of newborn hands
to hold these fragments
gold and honey most refined
erupts and flows
as molten magnet
down ducts of gaps
maternal magma sublime

I layer and layer the love
they stick to me
rich sturdy bits
dishevelled with mess and grit
on map of my cracks
they are bevelled worlds
continents on globe
moon and sun by which
whole vessel is lit
amphitheatre for story
that sits in the space I hold

and I funnel the crushed diamonds
of the memory of my mother's eyes
as she smiled
drizzling her dazzle
glaze drifts onto me like dreams
so if floored in my trials
her gemstones will still be sown
in newly grown seams

Acceptance is my defence
shatters the pretence
now I'm flattered by a true form
adorned in a loot beyond my gold
I transmute my history
let it pattern me bold

Kintsugi kisses
and moulds scars
into old friends
My form that shifts
is a gilded gift
I was in bits
Now reassembled
I ascend